BOUNTIFUL BLUE~BERRIES

Cookin' the Blues

by L. Hostetler

I

BOUNTIFUL BLUEBERRIES

© 2004 Lena Hostetler

All rights reserved. No part of this book may be reproduced or transmitted in any form or by any means, electronic or mechanical, except by a reviewer who may quote brief passages in a review to be printed in a magazine or newspaper.

HEARTS 'N TUMMIES COOKBOOK COMPANY
A Dinky Division of Quixote Press
1854-345th Avenue, Wever, IA 52658
1-800-571-BOOK

Blueberries are a good source of antioxidant activity, which can help lower the risk of cancer and heart disease, and even slow down some of the age-related brain deterioration. According to some recent research from the U.S. Department of Agriculture Human Nutrition Research Center on Aging at Tufts University, blueberries take the lead in a list of antioxidant-active fruits and vegetables.

Table of Contents

Sauces, Soups & Salads 6
Breads, Muffins, Etc. 18
Cookies & Cakes 52
Cobblers & Buckles 74
Pies 94
Other Desserts 124
Misc. 156

Sauces, Soups & Salads

Blueberries In Custard Sauce 8
Blueberry Glaze 9
Blueberry Topping 9
Blueberry Sauce 10
Blueberry Sauce Supreme 11
Blueberry Breakfast Sauce 12
Blueberry Honey Sauce 13
Easy Summer Salad 14
Blueberry Soup 16
Amish Blueberry Soup .16
Blueberry Salad 17

BLUEBERRIES IN CUSTARD SAUCE:

1 c. milk
1 egg, lightly beaten
2 T. sugar

pinch of salt
1/2 t. vanilla extract
3 c. blueberries

In saucepan, scald milk. Combine egg and sugar in a bowl; stir in small amount of hot milk. Return all to saucepan. Cook over low heat, stirring constantly, until mixture thickens slightly and coats a spoon, about 15 minutes. Remove from heat; stir in salt and vanilla. Chill at least 1 hour. Serve over blueberries. Yield: 6 servings.

BLUEBERRY GLAZE:

Microwave frozen blueberries with a little of your favorite fruit jelly or jam to make a thick, syrupy mixture. Top any cheesecake with the blueberry glaze.

BLUEBERRY TOPPING:

Let fresh or frozen blueberries stand in a mixture of sugar and lemon or lime juice until they release some of their juice. Spoon the berries over pound cake, angel food cake or ice cream.

BLUEBERRY SAUCE:

5 c. fresh blueberries	1 T. cornstarch
1 c. water	1 T. lemon juice
3/4 c. sugar	2 T. water

Combine blueberries, 1 cup water and sugar in large saucepan; bring to a boil. Combine 2 tablespoons water and cornstarch; mix well. Stir into blueberry mixture; cook 1 minute, stirring constantly. Remove from heat and add lemon juice; cool. Serve sauce over sponge cake, angel food cake, cheesecake etc.

BLUEBERRY SAUCE SUPREME:

1/2 c. sugar
1/4 c. orange juice
  concentrate

2 T. cornstarch
3 c. fresh or frozen
  blueberries

In a saucepan, combine sugar, orange juice concentrate and cornstarch; stir until smooth. Add blueberries and bring to a boil. Boil for 2 minutes, stirring constantly. Use as a topping for pancakes, waffles or pound cake. Yield: 2-1/4 cups.

BLUEBERRY BREAKFAST SAUCE

1/2 c. sugar
1 T. cornstarch
1/3 c. water

2 c. fresh or
frozen blueberries

In a 2 quart saucepan, combine sugar and cornstarch; gradually stir in water. Add blueberries; bring to a boil over medium heat, stirring constantly. Boil for 1 minute, stirring occasionally. Serve warm or cold over French toast, pancakes or waffles. Yield about 2 cups.

BLUEBERRY HONEY SAUCE:

2 c. blueberries
1 t. cinnamon
1/2 t. nutmeg

1/2 c. honey
1/4 c. butter
pinch of salt

In a saucepan combine all ingredients and bring to a boil. Reduce heat and simmer 5 minutes, stirring occasionally. Serve the sauce warm over ice cream, waffles, pancakes or french toast. Makes 1-1/2 cups.

EASY SUMMER SALAD:

1 (16 oz.) container cottage cheese
1 (8 oz.) container cool whip
1 (3 oz.) box jello (any flavor)
2 c. fresh or frozen blueberries
 or blueberry pie filling

Stir together cool whip, cottage cheese and dry jello. Then stir in the blueberries. Nuts and marshmallows may also be added, if desired. If using pie filling, Omit the jello.

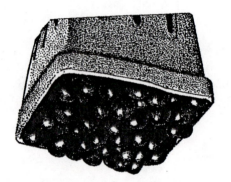

15

BLUEBERRY SOUP:

1/3 c. sour cream
10 oz. pkg. frozen blueberries,
  partially thawed

2 T. sugar
lemon slices, for
  garnish

Blend sour cream, blueberries and sugar in blender on low speed until smooth. Garnish with lemon slices. Serves 2.

AMISH BLUEBERRY SOUP:

Cube day old bread into a serving bowl. Sprinkle with sugar to taste. Add fresh, frozen or canned blueberries and milk to cover. stir all together and serve.

BLUEBERRY SALAD:

4 oz. cream cheese
3/4 c. powdered sugar
1/2 c. sour cream

1/2 t. lemon juice
1(8 oz.) ctn. cool whip

Mix cream cheese, powdered sugar, sour cream and lemon juice. Fold in cool whip and 2 pounds fresh blueberries.

Breads, Muffins, Etc.

Blueberry Pancakes 20
Blueberry French Toast .21
Blueberry Nut Bread 23
Blueberry Sour Cream Pancakes 25
Blueberry Coffee Cake 27
Blueberry Sour Cream Streusel Muffins 29
Berry Coffee Cake 31
Frozen Blueberry Muffins 33
Blueberry Buckle Coffee Cake 35

Buttermilk Blueberry Muffins 36
Lemon Blueberry Biscuits 37
Jam Filled Muffins 39
Overnight Blueberry Coffee Cake 40
Berry Mini Breads 41
Blueberry Streusel Coffee Cake 43
Blueberry Orange Muffins 45
Quick Blueberry Turnovers 46
Blueberry Tea Bread 47
Lemon Blueberry Bread 49
Goody Of Iowa 51

BLUEBERRY PANCAKES:

1-1/4 c. all-purpose flour
1 T. sugar
1 t. baking powder
1/2 t. baking soda
1/2 t. salt

1-1/4 c. buttermilk
2 T. vegatable oil
1 egg, beaten
1 c. fresh or frozen
  blueberries

In a bowl, combine flour, sugar, baking powder, baking soda and salt. In another bowl, combine buttermilk, oil and egg; stir into dry ingredients and mix well. Fold in blueberries. Pour by 1/4 cupfuls onto a lightly greased hot griddle; turn when bubbles form on top of pancakes. Cook until second side is golden brown. Yield: about 8 pancakes.

BLUEBERRY FRENCH TOAST:

12 slices day-old white
 bread, crusts removed
2 (8 oz.)pkgs. cream cheese
1 c. fresh or frozen blueberries
12 eggs
2 c. milk
1/3 c. maple syrup or honey

Sauce:
1 c. sugar
2 T. cornstarch
1 c. water
1 c. fresh or frozen
 blueberries
1 T. butter or margarine

Cut bread into 1-inch cubes; place half in a greased
13 x 9 x 2 inch baking dish. Cut cream cheese into 1-
inch cubes; place over bread. Top with blueberries and
remaining bread. In a large bowl, beat eggs. Add milk

and syrup; mix well. Pour over bread mixture. Cover and chill for 8 hours or overnight. Remove from refrigerator 30 minutes before baking. Cover and bake at 350 for 30 minutes. Uncover; bake 25-30 minutes more or until golden brown and center is set. In a saucepan, combine sugar and cornstarch; add water. Bring to a boil over medium heat; boil for 3 minutes, stirring constantly. Stir in blueberries; reduce heat. Simmer for 8-10 minutes or until berries have burst. Stir in butter until melted. Serve over french toast. Yield: 6-8 servings. (1-3/4 cups sauce)

BLUEBERRY NUT BREAD:

3 c. all-purpose flour	1 egg, beaten
1 c. sugar	1-2/3 c. milk
1 T. baking powder	1/4 c. cooking oil
1/4 t. baking soda	3/4 c. chopped almonds,
1/2 t. salt	pecans or walnuts
1 t. grated lemon peel	1 c. fresh or frozen
	blueberries

Grease the bottom and 1/2 inch up the side of a 9 x 5 x 3 inch loaf pan, set aside. In a large mixing bowl, stir together flour, sugar, baking powder, baking soda, and salt. Make a well in the center, set aside. In a medium mixing bowl, combine the egg, milk, lemon

peel and cooking oil. Add egg mixture all at once to dry mixture. Stir just until moistened. Fold in blueberries and nuts. Spoon batter into prepared pan. Bake at 350 for 1-1/4 hours or until a toothpick inserted near the center comes out clean. Cool in pan for 10 minutes. Remove loaf from pan. Cool completely on wire rack. Wrap and store overnight before slicing.
Yield: 1 loaf (18 servings).

BLUEBERRY SOUR CREAM PANCAKES:

1/2 c. sugar
2 T. cornstarch
1 c. water
4 c. fresh or frozen
  blueberries
    pancakes:
2 c. all-purpose flour
1/4 c. sugar
4 t. baking powder

1/2 t. salt
2 eggs
1-1/2 c. milk
1 c. sour cream
1/3 c. butter or
  margarine, melted
1 c. fresh or frozen
  blueberries

In a medium saucepan, combine sugar and cornstarch.
Gradually stir in water. Add blueberries; bring to a boil
over medium heat. Boil for 2 minutes, stirring constantly.

Remove from heat; cover and keep warm. For pancakes, combine dry ingredients in a bowl. In another bowl, beat the eggs. Add milk, sour cream and butter; mix well. Stir in dry ingredients just until blended. Fold in the blueberries. Pour batter by 1/4 cupfuls onto a greased hot griddle; turn when bubbles form on top of pancakes. Cook until the second side is golden brown. Serve with blueberry topping. Yield: about 20 pancakes.(3-1/2 cups topping).

BLUEBERRY COFFEE CAKE:

1-1/2 c. all-purpose flour	1/2 t. salt
1/2 c. sugar	1-1/2 c. fresh blueberries
1 t. baking powder	1 egg
1 t. baking soda	1/2 c. milk
1 t. cinnamon	1/4 c. margarine, melted

Topping:

1/4 c. margarine, melted	1 T. flour
3/4 c. packed brown sugar	1/2 c. chopped nuts

Need more!

Too Wet!

In a mixing bowl, combine the dry ingredients. Gently fold in blueberries. In a small bowl, whisk together the egg, milk and margarine. Add to the flour mixture and stir carefully. Spread into a greased 8 x 8 inch baking pan. Combine all topping ingredients until crumbs form. Sprinkle over batter. Bake at 425 for 25 minutes.

BLUEBERRY SOUR CREAM STREUSEL MUFFINS:

2 c. sifted all-purpose flour
2 t. baking powder
1/2 t. baking soda
1/2 t. salt
3 T. sugar
1 egg, well beaten
1 c. sour cream
1/3 c. milk

1/4 c. veg. oil
1-1/2 c. blueberries
1/2 c. brown sugar,
  firmly packed
1/4 c. all-purpose flour
1 t. ground cinnamon
3 T. butter or margarine

Sift 2 cups flour with baking powder, soda, salt and sugar. Beat egg with sour cream and milk. Stir in oil. Add liquids all at once to dry ingredients. Stir only until well blended. Carefully fold in blueberries. Spoon into greased muffin pans. Mix brown sugar, 1/4 c. flour and cinnamon. Cut in butter until crumbly and sprinkle over top of muffins. Bake at 425 for 15-25 minutes or until topping is a deep brown. Remove and cool on a rack. Serve warm or cold. Yield: **10-12** muffins.

BERRY COFFEE CAKE:

3 c. unsweetened blueberries
3 T. cornstarch
3 T. brown sugar
  Batter:
1 c. butter or margarine,
  softened
3/4 c. sugar
4 eggs
1 t. vanilla extract

2-1/2 c. all-purpose
  flour
1/2 t. baking powder
1/2 t. salt
  Glaze:
1 c. powdered sugar
1/4 t. vanilla extract
1-2 T. milk or water

In a saucepan, combine the blueberries, cornstarch and
brown sugar. Bring to a boil; cook and stir for 2 minutes

or until thickened. Cool slightly. In a mixing bowl, cream butter and sugar. Beat in eggs and extract. Combine the flour, baking powder and salt; add to creamed mixture and mix well. Set aside 1-1/2 cups for topping. Pour the remaining batter into a greased 15 x 10 x 2 inch baking pan. Top with blueberry filling; spoon reserved batter over the filling. Bake at 350 for 25 minutes or until a toothpick inserted near the center comes out clean. Combine the glaze ingredients and drizzle over coffee cake. Serve warm or at room temperature. Yield: 18-24 servings.

FROZEN BLUEBERRY MUFFINS:

4 c. all-purpose flour	4 eggs
4 t. baking powder	1 c. milk
1/2 t. salt	2 t. vanilla extract
1 c. butter or margarine, softened	2 c. frozen blueberries, unthawed
2 c. sugar	

TOPPING:

2 T. sugar	1/2 t. ground nutmeg

In a large bowl, combine the flour baking powder and salt. In a mixing bowl cream butter and sugar. Add eggs, milk and vanilla; mix well. Stir in the dry ingredients just until moistened. Fold in frozen blueberries.

Fill greased or paper lined muffin cups two-thirds full.
Combine sugar and nutmeg; sprinkle over muffins.
Bake at 375 for 20-25 minutes or until muffins test
done. Coolin pan for 10 minutes before removing
to a wire rack. Yield: about 2 dozen.

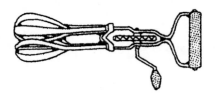

BLUEBERRY BUCKLE COFFEE CAKE:

4 c. all-purpose flour	1/2 c. shortening
1-1/2 c. sugar	1-1/2 c. milk
5 t. baking powder	2 eggs
1-1/2 t. salt	4 c. blueberries
Topping:	
2 c. sugar	1 t. ground cinnamon
2/3 c. all-purpose flour	1/2 c. margarine

Blend all the batter ingredients together except blueberries. Beat vigorously for 1/2 minute. Carefully stir in blueberries. Spread half of batter into a large greased baking pan. Mix topping ingredients together and sprinkle half over batter. Repeat layers and bake at 350 for 45-50 minutes.

BUTTERMILK BLUEBERRY MUFFINS:

2 c. all-purpose flour
1/2 c. packed brown sugar
1 T. baking powder
1 t. baking soda
1/2 t. grated lemon peel
1/2 t. ground nutmeg
1 c. blueberries
1 c. nonfat vanilla yogurt
1 c. buttermilk

In a large bowl, combine the first 6 ingredients. Gently fold in blueberries. Combine yogurt and buttermilk; stir into dry ingredients just until moistened. Fill greased or paper lined muffin cups two-thirds full. Bake at 400 for 18-20 minutes or until a toothpick comes out clean. Cool for 5 minutes before removing to a wire rack. Yield: 1 dozen.

LEMON BLUEBERRY BISCUITS:

2 c. all-purpose flour
1/3 c. sugar
2 t. baking powder
1/2 t. baking soda
1/4 t. salt
1 carton(8 oz.)lemon yogurt
1 egg, lightly beaten
1/4 c. butter or margarine, melted

1 t. grated lemon peel
1 c. fresh or frozen
  blueberries
Glaze:
 1/2 c. powdered sugar
 1 T. lemon juice
 1/2 t. grated lemon peel

In a large bowl, combine dry ingredients. Combine the
yogurt, egg, butter and lemon peel; stir into dry ingred-

ients just until moistened. Fold in blueberries. Drop by tablespoonfuls onto a greased baking sheet. Bake at 400 for 15-18 minutes or until lightly browned. Combine glaze ingredients; drizzle over warm biscuits. Makes about 1 dozen.

JAM FILLED MUFFINS:

1-3/4 c. all-purpose flour
1/2 c. sugar
1 T. baking powder
1/2 t. salt
2 eggs

2/3 c. milk
1/3 c. butter or
margarine, melted
1 t. grated lemon peel
1/2 c. blueberry jam

In a large bowl, combine flour, sugar, baking powder and salt. In a small bowl, lightly beat eggs; add milk, butter and lemon peel. Pour into dry ingredients and stir just until moistened. Spoon half of the batter into 12 greased or paper lined muffin cups. Make a well in the center of each; add jam. Spoon remaining batter over jam. Bake at 400 for 20 to 25 minutes or until golden. Yield: 1 dozen.

OVERNIGHT BLUEBERRY COFFEE CAKE:

1 egg
1/2 c. plus 2 T. sugar, divided
1-1/4 c. all-purpose flour
2 t. baking powder
3/4 t. salt
1/3 c. milk
3 T. butter or margarine, melted
1 c. fresh blueberries

In a mixing bowl, beat egg and 1/2 c. sugar. Combine flour, baking powder and salt; add alternately with milk to sugar mixture, beating well after each addition. Stir in butter. Fold in berries. Pour into a greased 8 inch square baking pan; sprinkle with remaining sugar. Cover and chill overnight. Remove from the refrigerator 30 minutes before baking. Bake at 350 for 30-35 minutes.

BERRY MINI BREADS:

1/2 c. butter or margarine,
  softened
1 c. sugar
2 eggs
3 c. all-purpose flour
1 t. baking soda
1 t. baking powder

1 t. salt
1 c. buttermilk
1 c. whole-berry
  cranberry sauce
1 c. fresh or frozen
  blueberries

In a mixing bowl, cream butter and sugar. Add eggs, one at a time, beating well after each addition. Combine dry ingredients; add to the creamed mixture alternately with buttermilk. Stir in cranberry sauce and blueberries. Pour into four greased 5-3/4 x 3 x 2 inch loaf pans. Bake at 350 for 25 to 30 minutes or until a toothpick inserted near the center comes out clean. Cool for 10 minutes before removing from pans to wire racks. Yield: 4 loaves.

BLUEBERRY STREUSEL COFFEE CAKE:

2 c. all-purpose flour
3/4 c. sugar
2 t. baking powder
1/4 t. salt
1 egg, beaten
1/2 c. milk
1/2 c. butter or margarine, softened

1 c. fresh or frozen blueberries
1 c. chopped pecans
Streusel:
1/2 c. sugar
1/3 c. all-purpose flour
1/4 c. cold butter or margarine

In a mixing bowl, combine flour, sugar, baking powder and salt. Add egg, milk and butter; beat well. Fold in blueberries and pecans. Spread into a greased 9-inch square baking pan. In another bowl, combine sugar and flour; cut in the butter until crumbly. Sprinkle over the batter. Bake at 375 for 35-40 minutes or until a toothpick inserted near the center comes out clean. Yield: 9 servings.

BLUEBERRY ORANGE MUFFINS:

1 c. oatmeal	1/2 t. baking soda
1 c. orange juice	1 c. sugar
3 c. all-purpose flour	1 c. cooking oil
4 t. baking powder	3 eggs, beaten
1 t. salt	2-3 c. blueberries

Mix oatmeal and orange juice. Combine with the rest of the ingredients, add blueberries last. Sprinkle sugar and cinnamon on top and bake at 400 for 15 minutes or until done.

2 doz

QUICK BLUEBERRY TURNOVERS:

1 tube(8 oz.)refrigerated crescent rolls
1 c. blueberry pie filling
1/2 c. powdered sugar
1-2 T. milk

Unroll dough and separate into eight triangles; Make four squares by pressing the seams of two triangles together and rolling into shape. Place on an ungreased baking sheet. Spoon 1/4 cup pie filling in one corner of each square. Fold to make triangles; pinch to seal. Bake at 375 for 10-12 minutes or until golden. Mix powdered sugar and milk; drizzle over turnovers. Serve warm. Yield: **4 servings.**

BLUEBERRY TEA BREAD:

2 c. all-purpose flour
1 c. sugar
1 T. baking powder
1/4 t. salt
1-1/2 c. fresh or frozen
  blueberries

1 t. grated orange peel
2 eggs
1 c. milk
3 T. vegetable oil
whipped cream cheese,
  optional

In a bowl, combine flour, sugar, baking powder and salt. Stir in blueberries and orange peel. In another bowl, beat eggs; add milk and oil. Stir into dry ingredients just until moistened. Pour into a greased 9 x 5 x 3 inch loaf pan. Bake at 350 for 1 hour or until a toothpick inserted near the center comes out clean. Cool in pan for 10 minutes; remove to a wire rack to cool completely. Serve with cream cheese if desired. Yield: 1 loaf.

LEMON BLUEBERRY BREAD:

1/3 c. butter or margarine, melted
1 c. sugar
2 eggs
3 T. lemon juice
1-1/2 c. all-purpose flour
1 t. baking powder
1/2 t. salt
1/2 c. milk
2 T. grated lemon peel
1/2 c. chopped nuts
1 c. fresh or frozen blueberries
Glaze:
2 T. lemon juice
1/4 c. sugar

In a mixing bowl, beat butter, sugar, eggs and juice. Combine flour, baking powder and salt; stir into egg mixture alternately with milk. Fold in peel, nuts and blueberries. Pour into a greased 8 x 4 inch loaf pan.

Bake at 350 for 60-70 minutes or until bread tests done. Cool in pan for 10 minutes. Meanwhile, combine glaze ingredients. Remove bread from pan and drizzle with glaze. Cool on a wire rack. Yield: 1 loaf.

GOODY OF IOWA:

1 c. sugar	1 egg
2 c. flour	1 c. milk
2 t. baking powder	1/4 c. butter

Mix dough and pour into pan.

2 c. blueberries	1 c. sugar
2 c. boiling water	

Mix & pour on top of dough. Bake at 400.

Cookies & Cakes

Blueberry-Filled Heart Cookies 53
Blueberry Sandwich Cookies 55
Peanut Butter 'N' Jelly Cookies 57
Blueberry Cheesecake 60
Blueberry Muffin Cakes 61
Blueberry Cake Cups 62
Blueberry Jelly Roll 63
Blueberry-Peach Pound Cake 65
Blueberry Cake 67
Blueberry Crunch Cake 69
Very Blueberry Cake 71
Blueberry Sponge Cakes 73

BLUEBERRY-FILLED HEART COOKIES:

1/2 c. butter or margarine,
  softened
1/2 c. shortening
1 c. sugar
1 egg
1/2 c. milk
1 t. vanilla extract

3-1/2 c. all-purpose
  flour
1 t. baking soda
2 t. baking powder
1/2 t. salt
blueberry jam

In a mixing bowl, cream the butter and shortening; gradually add sugar. Add egg, milk and vanilla. Combine dry ingredients; gradually add to creamed mixture. Mix well. Cover and refrigerate for at least 2 hours. Then roll out dough on a lightly floured surface to 1/8

inch thickness, cut with a 2-1/2 inch heart shaped cookie cutter dipped in flour. Place half of the cookies on greased baking sheets; spoon 1/2 t. jam in center of each. Use a 1-1/2 inch heart shaped cookie cutter to cut small hearts out of the other half of the cookies. (Bake small heart cutouts seperately.) Place the remaining hearts over filled cookies; press edges together gently. Fill centers with additional jam if needed. Sprinkle with additional sugar. Bake at 375 for 8-10 minutes or until lightly browned. Cool on wire racks.
Yield: About 4-1/2 dozen filled cookies.

BLUEBERRY SANDWICH COOKIES:

2 c. all-purpose flour
1 c. sugar
1 t. ground cinnamon
3/4 t. baking powder
1/4 t. salt
1/2 c. cold butter (no
  subtitutes)

1 egg
1/4 c. milk
2/3 c. blueberry jam
GLAZE:
  2 c. powdered sugar
  2 T. milk
  1/2 t. vanilla extract

In a large bowl, combine first five ingredients. Cut in butter until crumbly. In a small bowl, beat egg and milk. Add to crumb mixture just until moistened. Cover and refrigerate for 1 hour or until dough is easy to handle. On a lightly floured surface, roll out dough to 1/8 inch

thickness. Cut with a 2-inch round cookie cutter. Place on ungreased baking sheets. Bake at 375 for 8-10 minutes or until edges are lightly browned. Cool on wire racks. Spread jam on half of the cookies; top each with another cookie. In a small mixing bowl, combine sugar, milk and vanilla until smooth; spread over cookies.
Yield 2 dozen

PEANUT BUTTER 'N' JELLY COOKIES:

1/2 c. shortening
1/2 c. peanut butter
1/2 c. sugar
1/2 c. packed brown sugar
1 egg

1-1/4 c. all-purpose flour
3/4 t. baking soda
1/2 t. baking powder
1/4 t. salt
blueberry jam or jelly

In a mixing bowl, cream shortening, peanut butter and sugars. Beat in egg. Combine dry ingredients; gradually add to creamed mixture. Cover and chill for 1 hour. Roll into 1 inch balls; place 2 inches apart on greased baking sheets. Flatten slightly. Bake at 375 for 10 minutes or until golden brown. Cool on wire racks. Spread jam on the bottom of half of the cookies; top with remaining cookies. Yield: about 4-1/2 dozen.

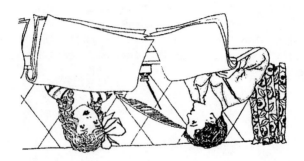

BLUEBERRY CHEESE CAKE:

1 pkg. white cake mix
2 (8 oz.) pkgs. cream cheese, softened
4 c. powdered sugar
1 pt. whipping cream, whipped
2 (21 oz.) cans blueberry pie filling

Prepare cake mix according to directions on package. Pour into two greased 9 x 13 x 2 inch baking pans. Bake at 350 for 20 minutes or until a toothpick inserted near the center comes out clean. Cool. In a mixing bowl, beat the cream cheese and sugar until fluffy; fold in the whipped cream. Spread over each cake. Top with pie filling. Chill 4 hours or overnight.
Yield: 24-30 servings.

BLUEBERRY MUFFIN CAKES:

1/2 c. shortening
3/4 c. sugar
2 eggs
2-1/3 c. all-purpose flour
1/2 t. salt
3/4 c. milk

2-1/2 t. baking powder
1/2 t. nutmeg
1 c. blueberries
1/2 c. melted butter
3/4 t. cinnamon
3/4 c. sugar

Cream shortening until light and fluffy. Gradually add sugar. Beat in eggs. Sift together, flour, baking powder, salt and nutmeg. Add alternately with milk, beginning and ending with dry ingredients. Fold in blueberries. Spoon dough into greased muffin pans, filling 3/4 full. Bake at 350 for 20 to 25 minutes. Remove cakes and cool slighty. Roll muffins in melted butter and then in sugar mixed with cinnamon.

BLUEBERRY CAKE CUPS:

1/4 c. all-purpose flour	1/4 c. milk
1/4 c. sugar	1 T. butter or
1/2 t. baking powder	margarine, melted
dash of salt	1 c. blueberries, divided

In a small bowl, combine flour, sugar, baking powder and salt. Stir in milk and butter just until moistened. Divide half of the berries between two greased 10-oz. custard cups. Top with batter and remaining berries. Bake at 375 for 25-30 minutes or until golden brown. Serve warm. Yield: 2 servings.

BLUEBERRY JELLY ROLL:

3 eggs
1/3 c. water
1 t. vanilla extract
1 c. cake flour
1/2 c. sugar

1 t. baking powder
1/4 t. salt
2/3 c. blueberry jelly
   or jam
powdered sugar

Heat oven to 375. Line a 15-1/2 x 10-1/2 x 1 inch jelly roll pan lined with waxed paper, grease. Beat eggs in a small bowl until thick and lemon colored, about 5 minutes. Pour eggs into a large mixer bowl, beat in sugar gradually. Blend in water and vanilla on low speed. Add flour, baking powder and salt gradually, beating until batter is smooth. Pour into pan, spreading batter to corners. Bake for 12-15 minutes or until a toothpick inserted near the center comes out clean. Loosen cake from edges of pan, invert on towel sprinkled with powdered sugar. Carefully remove paper. Roll up in towel while cake is still hot. When almost cool, unroll. Beat jelly slightly with fork to soften and spread over cake. Roll up, sprinkle with powdered sugar. Serves 10.

BLUEBERRY-PEACH POUND CAKE:

1/2 c. butter or margarine,
  softened
1-1/4 c. sugar
3 eggs
1/4 c. milk
2-1/2 c. cake flour
2 t. baking powder

1/4 t. salt
2-1/4 c. chopped peeled
  fresh peaches(1/2 in.
  pieces)
2 c. fresh or frozen
  blueberries
powdered sugar, optional

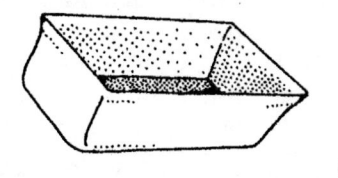

In a mixing bowl, cream butter and sugar. Beat in eggs, one at a time. Beat in milk. Combine the flour, baking powder and salt; add to creamed mixture. Stir in peaches and blueberries. Pour into a greased and floured 10-inch fluted tube pan. Bake at 350 for 60-70 minutes or until a toothpick inserted near the center comes out clean. Cool in pan for 15 minutes; remove to a wire rack to cool completely. Dust with powdered sugar if desired. Yield: 10-12 servings.

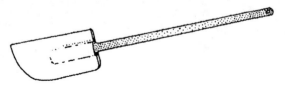

BLUEBERRY CAKE:

1 c. shortening	2 t. baking powder
2 c. sugar	1 t. salt
4 eggs	2/3 c. milk
2 t. lemon extract	2 c. blueberries
3 c. all-purpose flour	Additional sugar

In a large mixing bowl, cream shortening and sugar.
Beat in the eggs and lemon extract. Combine the flour,

baking powder and salt; gradually add to the creamed mixture alternately with milk. Fold in blueberries. Pour into a greased 9 or 10 inch tube pan. Sprinkle with additional sugar. Bake at 350 for 1 hour or until a tootkpick inserted near the center comes out clean. Cool for 10 minutes before removing from pan to a wire rack. Yield: 12-15 servings.

BLUEBERRY CRUNCH CAKE:

1/2 c. packed brown sugar
1/3 c. all-purpose flour
1/2 t. ground cinnamon
1/3 c. chopped pecans
1/3 c. cold butter
  Cake:
1/2 c. butter, softened
3/4 c. sugar

2 eggs
2 t. vanilla extract
2 c. all-purpose flour
2 t. baking powder
1/2 t. salt
3/4 c. milk
1-1/2 c. blueberries

In a bowl, combine the first four ingredients; cut in butter until crumbly. Set aside. In a mixing bowl, cream butter and sugar. Beat in eggs, one at a time. Stir in vanilla. Combine flour, baking powder and salt; add to the creamed mixture alternately with milk. Mix well. Spoon two-thirds of the batter into a greased 9 inch springform pan. Sprinkle with two-thirds of the crumb mixture. Top with blueberries and remaining batter and crumb mixture. Bake at 350 for 65-70 minutes or until a toothpick inserted near the center comes out clean. Cool for 10 minutes before removing sides of pan. Dust with confectioners' sugar. Yield: 8-10 servings.

VERY BLUEBERRY CAKE:

1/2 c. butter or margarine,
   softened
1/2 c. shortening
1-1/2 c. sugar
   Filling:
1 T. all-purpose flour
2 t. cornstarch
1 t. quick-cooking tapioca
   Glaze:
1 c. powdered sugar
1-2 T. milk

1 t. vanilla extract
1 t. almond extract
3 c. all-purpose flour
1/2 t. baking powder
2 eggs
4 c. fresh or frozen
   blueberries, divided
1 t. grated lemon peel

1 t. lemon juice

In a mixing bowl, cream butter, shortening and sugar. Beat in eggs, one at a time. Add extracts. Combine flour, and baking powder; add to creamed mixture and mix well. Spread two-thirds of the batter in a greased 15 x 10 x 1 inch baking pan. For filling, combine flour, cornstarch and tapioca in a large bowl. Add 1/2 cup of blueberries; mash with a fork and stir well. Add lemon peel and remaining blueberries; toss to coat. Pour evenly over batter in pan. Drop remaining batter by rounded tablespoonfuls over filling. Bake at 350 for 40 minutes or until golden brown. Combine glaze ingredients; drizzle over warm cake. Yield: 20 servings.

BLUEBERRY SPONGE CAKES:

1 individual prepared vanilla
  pudding cup(4 oz.)
1 t. vanilla extract
2 individual sponge cakes

1/2 c. blueberries
2 T. whipped topping
1 T. sliced almonds,
  toasted

In a small bowl, combine pudding and vanilla until
blended. Top each sponge cake with pudding and
berries. Dollop with whipped topping; sprinkle with
almonds. Yield: 2 servings.

Cobblers & Buckles

Blueberry Cobbler 76
Blueberry Cobbler 77
Berry Cobbler 79
Black And Blue Cobbler 81
Blueberry Buckle 83
Blueberry Grunt 85
Extra Easy Blueberry Cobbler 86
Blueberry Buckle 87
White Chocolate Blueberry Tart 89
Holiday Cheese Tarts 91
Fresh Blueberry Tarts 92
Blueberry Pudding Tarts 93

BLUEBERRY COBBLER:

3 c. blueberries
1/2 c. sugar
1-1/2 t. lemon juice
1 c. water
1/4 c. shortening

3/4 c. sugar
1-1/4 c. all-purpose flour
3 t. baking powder
1/4 t. salt
1/2 c. milk

Mix together blueberries, 1/2 cup sugar, lemon juice and water. Bring to boil and simmer for 5 minutes. Cream together 3/4 cup sugar and shortening, add rest of ingredients for dough. Mix until smooth. Pour batter into 10 x 15 inch baking pan. Spoon the blueberry mixture on top and bake at 350 for 45 minutes.

BLUEBERRY COBBLER:

6 c. blueberries	4-1/2 c. all-purpose
9 c. water	flour
3 c. sugar	1-1/2 t. salt
3 T. Real Lemon	2 T. baking powder
3 T. ground cinnamon	3 eggs
1 c. clear-jel	3/4 c. shortening
3 c. sugar	1 c. milk

In a large saucepan, combine water and 3 cups sugar and bring to a boil. Dissolve clear-jel in a little cold water and stir into boiling water. Bring to boil again. Remove from heat and add blueberries, Real Lemon and cinnamon. Put in bottom of two 9 x 13 inch baking pans. Mix together 3 cups sugar, flour, salt and baking powder. Add eggs, shortening and milk. Drop by tablespoon onto thickened blueberries. Bake at 350 for 40 minutes or until top springs back when lightly touched.

BERRY COBBLER:

4 c. fresh, frozen or
canned blueberries,
drained
1/2 c. sugar
2 T. lemon juice
1/8 t. nutmeg
2 T. melted butter or
margarine

1 c. all-purpose flour
2 t. baking powder
1 T. sugar
1/2 t. salt
1/4 c. shortening
1 egg, beaten
1/4 c. milk
1/4 t. cinnamon

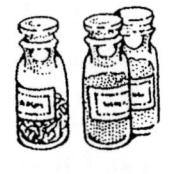

Combine berries with 1/2 cup sugar, lemon juice, nutmeg and butter or margarine. Place into greased double-boiler inset. In a seperate bowl, work shortening into dry ingredients until mixture looks like fine cornmeal. Mix together egg, milk and cinnamon and stir into dry ingredients using a fork. Spread batter over berries. Add 1 cup of water to a 3 quart saucepan and bring to a boil; place double-boiler inset in saucepan and cover. Cook over medium heat and, when vapor appears around edge of double-boiler, lower heat and cook 35 minutes. Serve cobbler hot, topped with fruit, cream, whipped cream, or vanilla ice cream. Serves 6.

BLACK AND BLUE COBBLER:

1 c. all-purpose flour
1-1/2 c. sugar, divided
1 t. baking powder
1/4 t. salt
1/4 t. ground cinnamon
1/4 t. ground nutmeg
2 eggs, beaten
2 T. milk

2 T. vegetable oil
2 c. fresh or frozen
  blueberries
2 c. fresh or frozen
  blackberries
3/4 c. water
1 t. grated orange peel

In a bowl, combine flour, 3/4 cup sugar, baking powder, salt, cinnamon and nutmeg. Combine eggs, milk and oil; stir into dry ingredients just until moistened. Spread the batter evenly onto the bottom of a greased 5-qt. slow cooker. In a saucepan, combine berries, water, orange peel and remaining sugar; bring to a boil. Remove from the heat; immediately pour over batter. Cover and cook on high for 2 to 2-1/2 hours or until a toothpick inserted near the center comes out clean. Turn cooker off. Uncover and let stand for 30 minutes before serving. Serve with whipped cream or ice cream if desired.
Yield: 6 servings.

BLUEBERRY BUCKLE:

1-1/4 c. sugar, divided
1/4 c. shortening
2 eggs
1/2 c. milk
1-1/2 c. all-purpose flour
2 t. baking powder
1/2 t. salt

1/2 t. ground nutmeg
1/4 t. ground cloves
2 c. blueberries
1/2 c. chopped nuts
1/4 c. softened butter
1/2 t. cinnamon
1/3 c. flour

Mix 3/4 c. sugar, shortening, eggs and milk until well blended. Stir in 1-1/2 cups flour, baking powder, salt, nutmeg and cloves. Fold in blueberries and spread batter into a 9-inch square pan. Combine remaining ingredients and mix until crumbly. Sprinkle crumbs over batter. Bake at 375 for 45-50 minutes or until top springs back when lightly touched. Cut in squares and serve with ice cream, whipped cream or cold milk. Yield: 9 servings.

BLUEBERRY GRUNT:

4 c. fresh blueberries
1 c. sugar
1 c. water
1-1/2 c. all-purpose flour
2 t. baking powder
2 t. grated orange peel

1/2 t. ground cinnamon
1/4 t. ground nutmeg
1/4 t. salt
3/4 c. milk
heavy cream, optional

In a skillet, combine blueberries, sugar and water; bring to a boil. Simmer uncovered for 20 minutes. In a bowl, combine the next six ingredients; stir in milk just until moistened (dough will be stiff). Drop by tablespoonfuls over blueberries. Cover and cook for 10-15 minutes or until dumplings are puffed and test done. Serve warm with cream if desired. Yield: 6-8 servings.

EXTRA EASY BLUEBERRY COBBLER:

- 4 c. blueberries
- 1 T. lemon juice
- 1 c. all-purpose flour (part whole wheat)
- 1 c. sugar
- 1 t. baking powder
- 1 egg, beaten
- 6 T. butter (melted)
- 1/4 t. ground cinnamon
- 1 T. brown sugar

Rinse berries and drain slightly. Place in bottom of 10 x 6 inch glass baking pan. Sprinkle with lemon juice. Mix flour, sugar, baking powder and egg with a fork until it resembles coarse corn meal. Distribute mixture over berries. Drizzle butter over top, then cinnamon and brown sugar. Bake at 350 for 35-40 minutes. Cobbler will thicken as it cools. Serve with cool whip, ice cream or milk.

BLUEBERRY BUCKLE:

1/4 c. butter or margarine,
3/4 c. sugar
2 eggs
1 t. vanilla extract
2-1/4 c. all-purpose flour,
   divided
2 t. baking powder
1/2 t. salt
1/2 c. buttermilk

2-1/2 c. fresh or frozen
   blueberries
Topping:
1/4 c. all-purpose flour
1/4 c. packed brown
   sugar
1/4 c. sugar
1/2 t. ground cinnamon
1/4 c. cold butter or
   margarine

In a mixing bowl, cream butter and sugar. Add eggs and vanilla; mix well. Combine 2 c. flour, baking powder and salt; add to creamed mixture alternately with buttermilk. Mix well. Toss berries in remaining flour; fold into batter (discard any flour that doesn't stick to berries). Spread batter in a greased 9-inch square baking pan. For topping, combine flour, sugars and cinnamon;cut in butter until the mixture resembles coarse crumbs. Sprinkle over batter. Bake at 375 for 25-30 minutes or until a toothpick inserted near the center comes out clean. Cool on a wire rack. Yield: 9 servings

WHITE CHOCOLATE BLUEBERRY TART:

3/4 c. butter, softened
1/2 c. confectioners sugar
1-1/2 c. all-purpose flour
1 pkg.(10-oz.)vanilla baking
  chips, melted
1 pkg.(8-oz.)cream cheese,
  softened

1/4 c. whipping cream
1 c. water
6 T. sugar
1 T. cornstarch
1 t. lemon juice
5-6 c. fresh blueberries

In a mixing bowl, cream butter and sugar. Gradually add flour; mix well. Press into an ungreased 11-inch tart pan or 12-inch pizza pan with sides. Bake at 300 for 25-30 minutes or until lightly browned. Cool. In a mixing bowl, beat chips and cream. Add cream cheese and beat until smooth. Spread over crust. Chill for 30 minutes. In a saucepan, sugar, cornstarch, lemon juice and water; bring to a boil over medium heat. Boil for 2 minutes or until thickened, stirring constantly. Cool; stir into blueberries and spread over filling. Chill one hour before serving. Yield: **12-16 servings**

HOLIDAY CHEESE TARTS:

1 (8 oz.) pkg. cream cheese, softened
1 (14 oz.) can Eagle Brand milk
1/3 c. lemon juice
1 t. vanilla extract

2 (4 oz.) pkgs. single serve graham cracker pie crusts
blueberries
1/4 c. apple jelly, melted (optional)

With mixer, beat cheese until fluffy. Gradually beat in sweetened condensed milk until smooth. Stir in lemon juice and vanilla. Spoon into crusts. Chill 2 hours or until set. Just before serving, top with blueberries; brush with jelly if desired. Makes 12 tarts.

FRESH BLUEBERRY TARTS:

- 1 pkg. (8 oz.) cream cheese, softened
- 1/4 c. packed light brown sugar
- 1 pkg. (6 count) individual graham cracker tart shells
- 2 c. fresh blueberries, divided
- 3 T. sugar
- 1 t. fresh lemon juice
- 1 t. grated lemon peel

In bowl, beat cream cheese and brown sugar until smooth. Spread in tart shells. In a bowl, mash 3 tablespoons blueberries with sugar, lemon juice and peel.

Add remaining berries and toss. spoon into tarts. Chill for 1 hour. Yield: 6 servings.

BLUEBERRY PUDDING TARTS:

Fill baked tart or tartlet shells with prepared vanilla pudding, and decorate the tops with a layer of blueberries. (If you use frozen blueberries, thaw and drain them first.)

Pies

Fluffy Lemon Blueberry Pie 96
Lemon Blueberry Pie 97
Blueberry Lattice Pie 99
Berry Best Fried Pies 101
Five Minute Blueberry Pie 103
Blueberry Cream Pie 104
Ozark Mountain Berry Pie 105
Quick Blueberry Pie 107
Two-Fruit Pie 107
Blueberry Topped Lemon Pie 108

Spiced Blueberry Crumble Pie 109
Blueberry Cheesecake Pie 111
Red White And Blue Berry Pie 113
Blueberry Cream Pie 115
Blueberry Pie 118
Fresh Blueberry Glaze 119
Easy Blueberry Cheese Pie 120
Blueberry Swirl Cheesecake Pie 121
Creamy Blueberry Pie 123

FLUFFY LEMON BLUEBERRY PIE:

- 1 (21 oz.) can blueberry pie filling
- 1 graham cracker pie crust
- 1 (8 oz.) pkg. cream cheese, softened
- 1 c. cold milk
- 1 (4 oz.) pkg. lemon instant pudding mix
- 1 (8 oz.) container cool whip, thawed

Spread half of the pie filling on bottom of crust. In a large bowl, beat cream cheese until smooth. Gradually beat in milk until well blended. Add pudding mix. Beat until smooth. Gently stir in half of cool whip. Spread over pie filling on bottom of crust. Spread remaining cool whip over pudding mixture. Top with remaining pie filling. Refrigerate 3 hours. Yield: 6-8 servings.

LEMON BLUEBERRY PIE:

6 eggs, lightly beaten
1 c. sugar
1/2 c. butter or margarine
1/3 c. fresh lemon juice
2 t. grated lemon peel

1(9 in.)baked pie crust
3 c. fresh blueberries
1/3 c. sugar
1/4 c. orange juice
1 T. cornstarch

In a saucepan, combine eggs, sugar, butter, lemon juice and peel; cook, stirring constantly, over medium-low heat until mixture thickens, about 20 minutes. Cool for 20 minutes, stirring occasionally. Pour into pie shell. In a saucepan, toss blueberries and sugar. Mix orange juice and cornstarch; add to blueberries. Cook over medium heat until mixture comes to a boil, about 8 minutes, stirring gently. Cook 2 minutes longer. Cool for 15 minutes, stirring occasionally. Spoon over lemon layer. Chill for 4-6 hours. Yield: 8 servings.

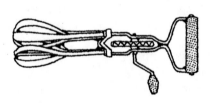

BLUEBERRY LATTICE PIE:

2 (9-in.)frozen pie shells,
  thawed to room temp.
3 c. fresh blueberries
1/2 c. sugar

2-1/2 T. cornstarch
1 T. butter
1/2 t. grated lemon peel
1 egg yolk

In a medium-sized saucepan, combine 1 cup of the blueberries, the sugar, cornstarch and 2 tablespoons water. Bring to a boil; cook and stir until mixture thickens and is clear. Stir in butter; cool for 5 minutes. Stir in the remaining 2 cups blueberries and lemon peel; cool. Preheat oven to 400. Pour cooled filling into one pie shell. Lay the remaining pie shell on a sheet of waxed paper;

press to close any cracks. With a knife or decorative pastry wheel, cut seven 3/4 inch wide strips; arrange in a criss-cross pattern on top of blueberries, pressing ends into the edges of the bottom crust. Combine egg yolk with 1 tablespoon water. Brush top crust with egg mixture. place pie on a baking sheet. Bake in the bottom third of the oven until crust is golden and filling gently bubbles, about 30 minutes. Cool on wire a rack; serve warm. Yield: 8 portions

BERRY BEST FRIED PIES:

1/2 c. sugar
1 T. cornstarch
1/2 c. water
    Dough:
2 c. all-purpose flour
1/4 t. baking soda
1/4 t. salt

2 c. fresh or frozen
   blueberries

1/2 c. vegetable oil
1/3 c. buttermilk
cooking oil for frying

In a saucepan, combine sugar, cornstarch and water; add berries. Cook and stir for 2 minutes; set aside to cool. Combine flour, baking soda and salt. Combine oil and buttermilk; stir into dry ingredients until mixture forms a ball. Roll on a floured board to 1/8 inch thickness; cut into 4-1/2 inch circles. Place 1 tablespoon blueberry filling on each circle. Fold over; seal edges with a fork. In a skillet over medium heat, fry pies in 1/4 to 1/2 inch hot oil until golden brown, about 1-1/2 minutes per side. Drain on paper towels. Yield: 10 servings.

FIVE MINUTE BLUEBERRY PIE

1/2 c. sugar
2 T. cornstarch
3/4 c. water
4 c. fresh or frozen
blueberries, thawed

1 graham cracker pie
crust (9 inch)
whipped cream,
optional

In a saucepan, combine sugar and cornstarch. Stir in water until smooth. Bring to a boil over medium heat, cook and stir for 2 minutes. Add blueberries. Cook for 3 minutes, stirring occasionally. Pour into crust. Chill. Garnish with whipped cream if desired.
Yield: 6-8 servings.

BLUEBERRY CREAM PIE:

4 oz. low-fat cream cheese, from an 8 oz. pkg., softened
1/2 c. low-fat sour cream
1/4 c. sugar
2 c. fresh blueberries, divided
1-1/2 c. nondairy whipped topping
1 (8-inch) graham cracker pie crust

In a medium bowl, with an electric mixer, beat cream cheese, sour cream and sugar until well blended. Fold in whipped topping. spoon half of the mixture into the pie crust; top with one cup of the blueberries. Spread remaining cheese mixture over the blueberries. Scatter the remaining 1 cup blueberries on top. Cover with plastic wrap, refrigerate until set, about 5 hours.

OZARK MOUNTAIN BERRY PIE:

1-1/2 c. sugar
4 T. plus 1-1/2 t. cornstarch
3/4 c. cold water
3 T. lemon juice

3 c. fresh blueberries
1 c. fresh raspberries
1 c. fresh blackberries
pastry for double-crust pie

In a saucepan, combine sugar and cornstarch. Stir in water and lemon juice until smooth. Add berries; stir gently. Bring to a boil over medium heat; cook and stir for 2 minutes or until thickened and bubbly. Remove from the heat; cool. Line a 9 inch pie plate with bottom crust. Add filling. Roll out remaining pastry; make a lattice crust. Seal and flute edges. Cover edges loosely with foil. Bake at 400 for 10 minutes. Reduce heat to 350. Remove foil; bake 40-50 longer or until crust is golden brown and filling is bubbly. Cool completely. Yield: 6-8 servings.

QUICK BLUEBERRY PIE:

Bake frozen puff pastry shells and fill them with lightly sweetened blueberries. Crown with whirls of whipped cream or whipped topping.

TWO-FRUIT PIE:

Mix blueberries with sliced apples or peaches, and add sugar and spices to make a delicious two-fruit pie filling. Serve the pie on it's own or a la mode.

BLUEBERRY TOPPED LEMON PIE:

3 egg yolks
1 (14 oz.) can sweetened condensed milk
1/2 c. lemon juice
1 (21 oz.) can blueberry pie filling
whipped topping
1 graham cracker pie crust

With mixer beat egg yolks and sweetened condensed milk until well blended. Stir in lemon juice. Pour into crust. Bake at 325 for 30 minutes. Chill at least four hours. Top with pie filling and garnish with whipped topping. Makes 1 pie.

SPICED BLUEBERRY CRUMBLE PIE:

4 c. fresh or frozen, thawed
   blueberries
1/2 c. sugar, divided
9 T. flour, divided
1/4 c. quick-cooking oats

1/4 c. walnuts, chopped
2 t. pumkin pie spice*
5 T. butter, cut in
   small pieces

Preheat oven to 375. In a 9-inch pie plate, toss blueberries with 1/4 cup sugar and 1 tablespoon of the flour; spread evenly in pie plate. In a medium bowl, combine remaining 8 tablespoons (1/2 cup) flour, the oats, walnuts, pumpkin pie spice and remaining 1/4 cup sugar. Using a pastry blender or two knives, cut in butter until moist crumbs form. With your fingers, press together crumbs to make large chunks; Place on top of blueberries. Bake in bottom third of oven until topping is browned, about 20 minutes; cool on a rack. Yield: 6 portions.

*To make your own blend, combine 1-1/4 teaspoons each ground cinnamon with 1/4 teaspoon each ground ginger, ground nutmeg and ground allspice.

BLUEBERRY CHEESECAKE PIE:

1 c. graham cracker crumbs
3 T. honey, divided
1 cont. (8 oz.) orange or tangerine yogurt
4 oz. low-fat cream cheese, from an 8 oz. package

3/4 c. nonfat cottage cheese
1 T. cornstarch
2 eggs
2 c. fresh blueberries

Preheat oven to 350. In a small bowl, combine graham cracker crumbs and 2 T. of the honey; transfer to a 9 in. pie plate. With the back of a spoon, press mixture onto bottom and halfway up sides of plate. In a food processor container, place yogurt, cream cheese, cottage cheese and cornstarch. Whirl until smooth, about 1 minute. Add eggs; whirl until blended. Pour about half of the cheese mixture onto the crust. Top with 1/2 cup of the blueberries. Cover with remaining cheese mixture. Bake until firm, about 35 minutes; cool on a wire rack. In a microwavable dish, microwave the remaining 1 tablespoon honey just until liquefied, about 15 seconds. Add the remaining 1-1/2 cups blueberries; toss to coat. Top pie with berries. Loosely cover pie; refrigerate until firm, about 3 hours. Yield 6 portions

RED WHITE AND BLUE BERRY PIE:

1-1/2 c. sugar
4-1/2 T. cornstarch
1-1/2 c. water
4-1/2 T. strawberry flavored
  gelatin
2 c. fresh or frozen
  unsweetened blueberries
1 t. lemon juice

1 pie crust(9 in.),baked
2 c. fresh or frozen
unsweetened strawberries
 4 oz. cream cheese
  softened
1/3 c. powdered sugar
4 oz. whipped topping,
  thawed

In a medium saucepan, combine sugar, cornstarch and water; cook and stir until thick and clear. Stir in gelatin until dissolved. Divide mixture in half. Stir blueberries and lemon juice into one half; spread in the bottom of the pie crust. Chill until set. Slice strawberries and stir into remaining gelatin; set aside at room temperature. In a mixing bowl, beat cream cheese and powdered sugar until smooth. Fold in whipped topping; spread over blueberry layer. Chill until set, about 2 hours. Carefully sread strawberry mixture over cream cheese layer. Chill for at least 4 hours. Yield: 8 servings.

BLUEBERRY CREAM PIE:

Crust:
1-1/3 c. vanilla wafer crumbs
5 T. butter or margarine,
    melted
        Filling:
1/4 c. sugar
3 T. all-purpose flour
pinch of salt
1 c. half-and-half cream
        Topping:
5 c. fresh blueberries,
    divided

2 T. sugar
1/2 t. vanilla extract

3 egg yolks, beaten
3 T. butter or margarine
1 t. vanilla extract
1 T. powdered sugar

2/3 c. sugar
1 T. cornstarch

Combine all crust ingredients; press into the bottom and sides of an ungreased 9-inch pie pan. Bake at 350 for 8-10 minutes or until crust just begins to brown. Cool. In a saucepan, combine sugar, flour and salt. Gradually whisk in cream; cook and stir over medium heat until thickened and bubbly. Cook and stir 2 minutes more. Gradually whisk half into egg yolks; return all to pan. Bring to a gentle boil; cook and stir 2 minutes. Remove from heat; stir in butter and vanilla until butter is melted. Cool for 5 minutes, stirring occasionally. Pour into crust; sprinkle with powdered sugar. Chill 30 minutes or until set. Meanwhile, crush 2 cups of blueberries in a medium saucepan; bring to a boil. Boil 2 minutes stirring constantly. Press berries through sieve; set aside 1 cup juice (add water if necessary). Discard pulp. In a

saucepan, combine sugar and cornstarch. Gradually stir in blueberry juice; bring to a boil. Boil 2 minutes, stirring constantly. Remove from heat; cool 15 minutes. Gently stir in remaining berries; carefully spoon over filling. Chill 3 hours or until set. Store in refrigerator.
Yield: 6–8 servings

BLUEBERRY PIE:

3/4 c. sugar
1 c. sweet cream
3 T. all-purpose flour

1/2 t. ground cinnamon
dash of salt
2 c. fresh blueberries

Mix all together and pour into an unbaked pie shell.
Bake at 350 until done.

FRESH BLUEBERRY GLAZE:

2-1/2 c. water
2 c. sugar
1/2 c. fresh blueberries
1/2 c. sugar

3/4 c. clear-jel
1 t. lemon juice
1/2 t. salt
3/4 c. water

Mix first three ingredients together in a saucepan and bring to a boil. Mix remaining ingredients and add to boiling mixture. Cook until clear. Add 1 cup canned blueberry pie filling when mixture is cold. Add 6-2/3 cups fresh blueberries and pour into baked pie shells. Top with whipped topping. Makes 3 pies.

EASY BLUEBERRY CHEESE PIE:

1 (8 oz.) pkg. cream cheese, softened
1 (14 oz.) can Eagle Brand sweetened condensed milk
1 t. vanilla extract
blueberry pie filling
1/3 c. lemon juice

In a medium bowl, beat cream cheese until light and fluffy. Add condensed milk, blend thoroughly. Stir in lemon juice and vanilla. Pour into a baked pie crust and chill for 2 hours or until set. Top with desired amount of pie filling before serving.

BLUEBERRY SWIRL CHEESECAKE PIE:

pastry for single-crust
  pie (9-in.)
2 (8 oz.) pkgs. cream
  cheese, softened
1/2 sugar

1 t. vanilla extract
2 eggs
3 T. blueberry jam
whipped topping (optional)

Line unpricked pastry shell with a double thickness of
heavy-duty foil. Bake at 450 for 5 minutes; remove
from the oven; reduce heat to 350. In a mixing bowl,
beat cream cheese, sugar and vanilla until smooth.
Add eggs, beating on low speed just until combined.

Pour into pastry shell. Stir jam; drizzle over the filling. Cut through the filling with a knife to swirl the jam. Bake for 25 to 30 minutes or until center is almost set. Cool on a wire rack for 1 hour. Refrigerate overnight. Let stand at room temperature for 30 minutes before slicing. Garnish with whipped topping if desired.

CREAMY BLUEBERRY PIE:

1 (8 oz.) pkg. cream cheese, softened
1 c. whipping cream
1/4 c. sugar
1 t. lemon juice

1 (21 oz.) can blueberry pie filling
1 baked pie crust
additional whipped cream, if desired

Beat cream cheese until light and fluffy. In another bowl, beat whipping cream, sugar and lemon juice until soft peaks form. Beat cream mixture into cream cheese until smooth and spoon into crust. Chill or freeze. If frozen remove from freezer 15 minutes before serving. Garnish with additional whipped cream if desired. Makes 1 pie.

Other Desserts

Blueberry Butterscotch Squares	126
Blueberry Citrus Bars	127
Very Berry Melba	129
Peanut Butter And Jelly Bars	131
Blueberry Oat Bars	133
Blueberry Cream Cheese Squares	135
Frozen Blueberry Cheesecake	137
Blueberry Bars	138
Blueberry Custard Parfait	139
Shortcake Squares	141

Blueberry Bombe 143
Blueberry Angel Dessert 145
Blueberry Yogurt 146
Delightful Blueberry Dessert 147
Blueberry Swirls 149
Layered Blueberry Dessert 151
Lady Finger Trifle 152
Easy Filled Drops 153
Blueberry On A Cloud 155

BLUEBERRY BUTTERSCOTCH SQUARES:

1-1/2 c. flour
1/2 t. salt
1/4 t. soda
3/4 c. sugar
2 eggs

1-1/2 c. blueberries
1 c. butterscotch chips
1/2 c. chopped pecans
2 T. brown sugar

Mix flour, salt and soda. Cream margarine until light and fluffy. Gradually add sugar. Beat in eggs, stir in dry ingredients and fold in blueberries. Spread into a 13 x 9 x 2 inch baking pan. Sprinkle with chips, pecans and brown sugar. Bake at 350 for 30 minutes or until top is lightly browned. Cool in pan and cut in squares.

BLUEBERRY CITRUS BARS:

1 c. (2 sticks) butter, softened
3/4 c. sifted powdered sugar
2-1/4 c. unsifted flour
1/2 c. finely chopped pecans
4 eggs
1-1/2 c. sugar
1 c. ReaLemon juice
1 t. baking powder
1-1/2 c. fresh or frozen blueberries, thawed

Beat butter in medium-sized bowl with mixer until fluffy. Add powdered sugar; beat until combined. Beat in two cups of the flour. Stir in 1/4 cup of the pecans. Press on bottom of 13 x 9 inch greased baking pan. Bake at 350 for 20 minutes or until golden. Meanwhile, for filling, combine eggs, sugar, ReaLemon, baking powder and remaining 1/4 cup flour in large bowl. Beat with mixer on medium speed 2 minutes. Sprinkle berries over prepared crust. Top with filling and remaining 1/4 cup pecans. Bake 30-35 minutes longer or until set and top is lightly golden. Cool. Sift additional powdered sugar over top. Cut into bars. Store leftovers covered in refrigerator. Makes 24-36 bars.

VERY BERRY MELBA:

1/2 gal. vanilla ice cream,
 softened
1/4 c. orange juice concentrate
1-1/2 t. ground cinnamon
3 c. fresh or frozen blueberries

2 c. fresh or frozen
 raspberries
1 T. lemon juice
2 T. cornstarch

In a bowl, combine ice cream, orange juice concentrate and cinnamon. Cover and freeze for 2-3 hours or until firm. Meanwhile, combine berries and lemon juice in a saucepan; cover and cook over low heat for 10 minutes, stirring occasionally. Combine sugar and cornstarch; Stir into berry mixture. Bring to a boil over medium heat; boil for 2 minutes, stirring constantly. Remove from heat. Cool; cover and refrigerate. To serve, spoon ice cream into a bowl or parfait glass; top with berry sauce.

PEANUT BUTTER AND JELLY BARS:

1/2 c. sugar
1/2 c. brown sugar
1/2 c. shortening
1/2 c. peanut butter
1 egg
1-1/4 c. all-purpose flour
3/4 t. baking soda
1/2 t. baking powder

1/2 c. blueberry jelly or jam
Glaze:
1 c. powdered sugar
2 t. margarine, melted
1 t. vanilla extract
1 T. hot water

Cream sugars, shortening, peanut butter and egg. Stir in dry ingredients. Reserve 1 cup dough. Press remaining dough in 13 x 9 inch ungreased baking pan. Spread with jelly. Crumble remaining dough and sprinkle over jelly. Bake at 350 for 20 minutes. Mix glaze ingredients and drizzle over bars.

BLUEBERRY OAT BARS:

1-1/2 c. all-purpose flour
1-1/2 c. quick-cooking oats
1-1/2 c. sugar, divided
1/2 t. baking soda
3/4 c. cold butter or margarine

2 c. fresh or frozen
  blueberries
2 T. cornstarch
2 T. lemon juice

In a bowl, combine flour, oats, 1 cup sugar and baking soda. Cut in butter until mixture resembles coarse crumbs. Reserve 2 cups for topping. Press remaining crumb mixture into a greased 13 x 9 x 2 inch baking pan; set aside. In a saucepan, combine blueberries, cornstarch lemon juice and remaining sugar. Bring to a boil; boil for 2 minutes, stirring constantly. Spread evenly over the crust. Sprinkle with the reserved crumb mixture. Bake at 375 for 25 minutes or until lightly browned. Cool before cutting. Yield: 2-1/2 to 3 dozen.

BLUEBERRY CREAM CHEESE SQUARES:

1/4 c. cornstarch
1/2 c. sugar
1/2 c. water
2/3 c. blueberries, rinsed
and drained
1-1/2 sticks butter or
margarine, melted

2 c. graham cracker
crumbs
2 (8-oz.)pkgs. cream
cheese, softened
1/2 c. sugar
2 t. vanilla extract
3/4 c. cream, whipped

Combine cornstarch, sugar, water and blueberries and
cook over medium heat, stirring constantly until it
thickens. Cool. Combine graham cracker crumbs and
melted butter. Press two-thirds of crumb mixture in
bottom of a 9 x 12 x 2 inch pan, saving the remaining
crumbs for the top. Mash cream cheese until soft, grad-

ually beat in sugar and vanilla. Fold in whipped topping. Spread half of cream cheese mixture carefully over crumbs. Spread cooled blueberry filling evenly over cream cheese layer. Then spread remaining cheese mixture over this. Top with remaining crumbs. Refrigerate overnight before serving.

FROZEN BLUEBERRY CHEESECAKE:

Crust:

2 pkgs. graham crackers,
crushed

6 T. brown sugar
3/4 c. melted butter

Filling:

2 (8 oz.)pkgs. cream cheese
1 c. sugar
1 c. Rich's topping, whipped

4 eggs, well beaten
1 t. vanilla extract

Mix crust ingredients and press into bottom of 9 x 13 inch pan. Mix together the rest of the ingredients and pour over graham cracker crust and freeze. Remove from freezer 15–30 minutes before serving. Serve with thickened blueberries.

BLUEBERRY BARS:

1 c. all-purpose flour
1/2 c. sugar
1/2 c. butter

Mix and spread in 8 inch square baking pan. Cover lightly with blueberry jam.

Topping:
1 c. brown sugar
1/2 c. butter
1 egg
2 c. coconut
1 t. vanilla extract

Mix all together and spread over jam. Bake at 350 for 30 minutes or until toothpick comes out clean.

BLUEBERRY CUSTARD PARFAIT:

2 eggs, lightly beaten
1-1/2 c. milk
1/4 c. sugar
1/4 t. salt
1 t. vanilla extract
1 t. grated orange peel

1 t. grated lemon peel
1/4 t. ground nutmeg
1/2 c. heavy cream
2 t. powdered sugar
2 c. fresh blueberries

In a saucepan, combine eggs, milk, sugar and salt. Cook over medium-low heat, stirring constantly, until custard is slightly thickened and coats the back of a spoon, about 18 minutes. Remove from the heat. Add vanilla, peels and nutmeg; mix well. Cool for 30 minutes, stirring occasionally. In a small mixing bowl, whip the cream and powdered sugar until stiff. Fold two-thirds into the custard. Layer custard and blueberries in parfait glasses. Garnish with remaining cream. Chill for 1 hour. Yield: 4 servings.

SHORTCAKE SQUARES:

2 c. all-purpose flour
1 T. baking powder
1 T. sugar
1/2 t. salt
1/3 c. shortening
1 egg

1/2 c. milk
2 T. butter or margarine,
 softened
sweetened blueberries
whipped cream

In a bowl, combine flour, baking powder, sugar and salt; cut in shortening until mixture resembles coarse crumbs. In a bowl, whisk the egg and milk until well blended; add to dry ingredients. Stir with a fork just until moistened. pat into a greased 9-inch square baking pan. Bake at 375 for 18-20 minutes or until golden brown. Cool on a wire rack. Cut into squares. Split each square horizontally and butter the sides. Top with berries and whipped cream. Yield: 9 servings.

BLUEBERRY BOMBE:

1 envelope Knox Gelatine
1/2 c. cold milk
1 c. milk, heated to boiling
1 pkg.(12 oz.) frozen unsweetened blueberries, rinsed

1/4 c. sugar
2 c. frozen whipped
   topping, thawed

In a blender, sprinkle Knox gelatine over cold milk; let stand 2 minutes. Add hot milk and process at low speed until gelatine is completely dissolved, about 2 minutes. Add blueberries and sugar; process until blended, about 1 minute. Pour into large bowl, then with wire whisk blend in whipped topping. Pour into 8 dessert cups; chill until firm, about 3 hours. Garnish, if desired with additional whipped topping and grated lemon peel. Makes about 8 (1/2 cup) servings.

FOR A REFRESHING FROZEN BOMBE: Freeze individual dessert cups 3 hours or until firm. To serve let stand at room temperature 15 minutes or until slightly softened. Garnish as above.

BLUEBERRY ANGEL DESSERT:

1 pkg.(8 oz.) cream cheese, softened
1 c. confectioners sugar
1 carton (8 oz.) frozen whipped topping, thawed
1 prepared angel food cake(14 oz.)cut into 1-in. cubes
2 cans (21 oz. each) blueberry pie filling

In a large mixing bowl, beat the cream cheese and sugar; fold in whipped topping and cake cubes. Spread evenly into an ungreased 13 x 9 x 2 inch dish; top with pie filling. Cover and refrigerate for at least 2 hours before cutting into squares. Yield: 12-15 servings.

BLUEBERRY YOGURT:

6 c. whole milk
1 pkg. unflavored gelatin
fresh blueberries

1/4 c. yogurt (plain)
1/3 c. sugar (optional)
1/4 c. water

Heat milk to almost boiling. Remove from heat; add gelatin that has been dissolved in water and sugar. Cool to lukewarm and add yogurt. Beat together, then pour into yogurt maker or set on top of refrigerator until thickened (about 12 hours). Stir in desired amount of blueberries. For extra flavor, mix 1 small pkg. lemon or black raspberry jello with 1/2 the amount water it calls for on package and beat in before adding blueberries. Then chill until it thickens.

DELIGHTFUL BLUEBERRY DESSERT:

3 egg whites
1-1/2 c. sugar, divided
3/4 t. cream of tartar
1/2 c. crushed saltines
(about 15 crackers)

1/2 c. flaked coconut
1/2 c. chopped pecans
2 c. whipping cream
1/2 t. unflavored gelatin
4 c. fresh blueberries

In a mixing bowl, beat egg whites until soft peaks form. Gradually add 1 cup sugar and cream of tartar, beating until stiff peaks form. Gently fold in crumbs, coconut and pecans. Spread onto the bottom and up the sides of a 9-inch pie plate. Bake at 375 for 20-22 minutes or until lightly browned. Cool completely. In a mixing bowl, beat cream, gelatin and remaining sugar until stiff peaks form. Fold in blueberries; pour into shell. Refrigerate for 2 hours. Yield: 10-12 servings.

BLUEBERRY SWIRLS:

1 c. butter(no substitutes),
   softened
2 c. sugar
2 eggs
1 t. vanilla extract
1/2 t. lemon extract

3-3/4 c. all-purpose
   flour
2 t. baking powder
1 t. salt
1-1/2 c. blueberry jam
1 c. flaked coconut
1/2 c. chopped pecans

In a mixing bowl, cream butter and sugar. Add the eggs
and extracts; mix well. Combine flour, baking powder
and salt; add to creamed mixture and mix well. Cover
and chill for at least 2 hours. Divide dough in half. On
a lightly floured surface, roll each half into a 12 x 9 in.

rectangle. Combine jam, coconut pecans; spread over rectangles. Carefully roll up starting with the long end, into a tight jelly roll. Wrap in plastic wrap. Refrigerate overnight or freeze for 2-3 hours. Unwrap and cut into 1/4 inch slices; Place on greased baking sheets. Bake at 375 for 10-12 minutes or until lightly browned. Cool 2 minutes before removing to wire racks to cool completely. Yield: 8 dozen.

LAYERED BLUEBERRY DESSERT:

First layer:
2 c. all-purpose flour
1 c. butter or margarine,
  melted
  Second layer:
1(8 oz.)pkg. cream cheese,
  softened

1/2 c. brown sugar
1 c. chopped pecans

1 c. powdered sugar
1(8 oz.)ctn. cool whip

Combine first layer ingredients; spread in 9 x 13 inch baking pan. Bake at 375 for 15 minutes; cool. Beat cream cheese and powdered sugar until smooth. Fold in cool whip and spread on first layer. Top with blueberry pie filling, sauce or danish dessert.

LADY FINGER TRIFLE:

2 (one 8-oz., one 3-oz.) pkgs. cream cheese, softened
1 c. powdered sugar
2 c. whipping cream, whipped
1 (3-oz.) pkg. ladyfingers
1 (21-oz.) can blueberry pie filling

In a mixing bowl, beat cream cheese and sugar until smooth. Fold in whipped cream. Split lady fingers; arrange upright around the edge and over the bottom of a 2 quart serving bowl (about 8-inch diameter). Pour cream cheese mixture into bowl. Cover and refrigerate for 4 hours or overnight. Just before serving, spoon pie filling over cream cheese mixture. Yield: 8-10 servings.

EASY FILLED DROPS:

1 c. shortening
2 c. brown sugar
2 eggs
1/2 c. water, sour milk, or
 buttermilk
1 t. vanilla extract

3-1/2 c. sifted flour
1 t. salt
1 t. baking soda
1/8 t cinnamon
 blueberry jam

Heat oven to 400. Mix well; shortening, sugar and eggs. Stir in water and vanilla. Sift dry ingredients together and stir into other mixture. Drop with teaspoon onto ungreased baking sheet. Place 1/2 teaspoon blueberry jam on dough, cover with 1/2 teaspoon dough. Bake 10-12 minutes. Makes 5 to 6 dozen.

BLUEBERRY ON A CLOUD:

3 egg whites
1/4 t. cream of tartar
3/4 c. sugar
blueberry pie filling

1 c. cream, whipped
8 oz. cream cheese
1 c. minature marshmallows
1/2 c. powdered sugar

In a mixing bowl, beat egg whites and cream of tartar until very stiff. Beat in the sugar, 1 tablespoon at a time. Spread in 9 x 13 inch baking pan. Bake at 275 for 1-1/2 hour. Turn oven off but leave in oven at least 1 hour longer. Stir the powdered sugar and softened cream cheese together until smooth. Fold in whipped cream and marshmallows. Spread over crust. Top with pie filling or thickened fresh blueberries.

Misc.

Fresh And Easy Berry Jam 158
Blueberry Jelly 159
Blueberry Pie Filling To Can 161
Blueberry Pie Filling To Can 162
Blueberry Jam 163
Blueberry Smoothie 165
Blueberry Drink 166
Blueberry Omelet 167
Blueberry Freezer Jam 169
Freezing Blueberries 171
Canning Blueberries 171

FRESH AND EASY BERRY JAM:

2 envelopes unflavored gelatine	1/2 c. sugar*
1 c. cold water	1/4 c. lemon juice
	4-1/2 c. blueberries

In a large saucepan, sprinkle gelatine over cold water; let stand 1 minute. Stir over low heat until gelatine is completely dissolved, about 5 minutes. Add blueberries, sugar and lemon juice. Bring to a boil, then simmer, stirring occasionally and crushing berries slightly, 10 minutes. Spoon into jars; cool slightly before refrigerating. Chill until set, about 3 hours. Store up to 4 wks. in refrigerator or up to 1 year in freezer. Makes 4 cups.
*Use more or less sugar according to ripeness of berries.

BLUEBERRY JELLY:

2 qt. fresh or frozen
  blueberries
4 c. water

12 c. sugar
2 (3 oz.) pouches
  liquid fruit pectin

Place blueberries in a large kettle and crush slightly. Add water; bring to a boil. Reduce heat to medium; cook, uncovered for 45 minutes. Strain through a jelly bag, reserving 6 cups juice. Pour juice into a large kettle; gradually stir in sugar until dissolved. Bring to a boil over high heat, stirring constantly. Add pectin; bring to a full rolling boil. Boil for 1 minute stirring constantly. Remove from the heat. Skim foam. Pour hot into sterilized hot jars, leaving 1/4-inch headspace. Adjust caps. Process for 5 minutes in a boiling-water bath. Yield: 6 pints.

BLUEBERRY PIE FILLING TO CAN:

9-1/2 c. water
4-1/2 c. sugar

1 c. clear jel or
cornstarch

Heat sugar and 8 cups water to boiling. In small bowl mix cornstarch with remaining 1-1/2 cup water. Add to boiling water, stirring constantly until thickened. Stir in 7 quarts blueberries and ladle in glass canning jars, leaving at least 1 inch head space. If jars are too full, syrup will spew out during processing. Tighten lids and process in boiling water bath for 20 minutes. You may want to add 1 teaspoon lemon juice per quart when ready to use.

BLUEBERRY PIE FILLING TO CAN:

6 c. water
6 c. sugar
2 c. permaflo

1-1/2 c. water
6 qt. blueberries

Boil 6 cups water and sugar 1 minute. Mix permaflo with 1-1/2 cup water. Add to boiling water. Bring to a boil stirring constantly until thick and clear. Remove from heat and add blueberries. Put in jars leaving at least 1 inch head space so it won't spew out while processing. Process in boiling water bath for 20 minutes.

Note: If you use permaflo for your thickener, your filling will stay nice and clear and will not seperate when canned.

BLUEBERRY JAM:

3 pt. blueberries
2 T. lemon juice

4 c. sugar
1 box Sure-Jell

Crush berries 1 cup at a time with potato masher to make 4 cups crushed berries. Place in 6 or 8 qt. saucepot. Add lemon juice. Measure sugar (very accurately) and set aside. Stir Sure-Jell into blueberries. Add 1/2 teaspoon. butter or margarine(to prevent foaming while cooking). Bring to a full boil (one that does not stop when stirred) over high heat, stirring constantly. Add sugar quickly and return to full rolling boil. Boil hard exactly 1 minute stirring constantly. Remove from heat. Skim off any foam. Fill hot sterilized jars quickly to 1/8 inch of tops. Wipe jar rims and threads. Cover quickly with flat lids. Screw bands tightly. Invert jars 5 minutes, then turn upright. After jars are cool, Check seals by pressing middle of lid with finger. If lid springs up when finger is released, lid is not sealed. Let stand at room temperature 24 hours. Store unopened jars in cool, dry, dark place up to 1 year, or in refrigerator up to 3 wks. (Or leave 3/4 inch space at top, and process in boiling water bath for 5 minutes.)

BLUEBERRY SMOOTHIE:

1 c. fresh or frozen blueberries   1 c. milk
 honey to taste   ice cubes
1 t. vanilla extract

Blend all together in a blender.

BLUEBERRY DRINK:

Whirl frozen blueberries, banana chunks and orange juice in a blender to make a nutritious drink for breakfast or an afternoon pick-me-up.

BLUEBERRY OMELET:

1 T. butter or margarine	1/2 t. salt
4 eggs	1/8 t. pepper
4 T. water	1/3 c. blueberry jam

Place butter in 9-inch microproof pie plate. Use COOK cycle and cook 30 seconds, or until melted. In small bowl, beat remaining ingredients, except jam, with a fork. Pour into pie plate. Cover with waxed paper. Use COOK cycle and cook 3 minutes, stirring once during cooking time. Cover. Use COOK cycle and cook 1 to 1-1/2 minutes; stir. Let stand, covered, 1 to 2 minutes. Spread jam over half of omelet; fold other half over

jam. Cut in half. Serve hot. Makes 2 servings.
  You can also make this in a heavy skillet on top of the stove.

BLUEBERRY FREEZER JAM:

2-1/2 pt. blueberries
5-1/4 c. sugar
3/4 c. water

1 box Sure-Jell fruit
    pectin

Crush berries 1 cup at a time to make 3 cups crushed berries. Put into a large bowl. Measure sugar into a medium bowl. (Scrape excess sugar from cup with spatula to level for exact measure.) Stir sugar into berries. Set aside for 10 minutes; stir occasionally. Stir Sure-Jell and water in small saucepan. (It may be lumpy before cooking.) Bring mixture to boil on high heat, stirring constantly. Boil and stir 1 minute. Remove from heat. Stir pectin mixture into berry mixture. Stir constantly until sugar is completely dissolved and no longer grainy, about 3 minutes. (A few sugar crystals may remain.) Pour quickly into clean plastic containers to within 1/2 inch of tops. Wipe off top edges of containers; cover with lids. Let stand at room temperature for 24 hours to set. For immediate use, store in refrigerator up to 3 weeks. Freeze remaining containers up to 1 year. To use, thaw in refrigerator. Yield: approximately 7 cups.

FREEZING BLUEBERRIES:

Spread unwashed dry blueberries on a baking sheet and put them in the freezer until completely frozen. Store in freezer containers. Rinse before using.

CANNING BLUEBERRIES:

For each quart, dissolve 1/2 cup sugar in 1/2 cup hot water. Fill cans with blueberries; pour sugar mixture over blueberries. If cans aren't full add more water. Process in hot water bath for 5 minutes. Use more or less sugar to taste.

NEED GIFTS?

Are you up a stump for some nice gifts for some nice people in your life? Here's a list of some of the best cookbooks in the western half of the Universe. Just check 'em off, stick a check in an envelope with this page, and we'll get your books off to you pronto. Oh, yes, add $2.00 for shipping and handling for the first book and then fifty cents more for each additional one. If you order over $30.00, forget the shipping and handling.

Mini Cookbooks
(Only 3 1/2 x 5) With Maxi Good Eatin' - 160 or 192 pages - $5.95

- ☐ Arizona Cooking
- ☐ Dakota Cooking
- ☐ Illinois Cooking
- ☐ Indiana Cooking
- ☐ Iowa Cookin'
- ☐ Kansas Cookin'
- ☐ Kentucky Cookin'
- ☐ Cooking with Things Go Baa
- ☐ Cooking with Things Go Cluck
- ☐ Cooking with Things Go Moo
- ☐ Cooking with Things Go Oink
- ☐ Cooking with Things Go Splash
- ☐ Cooking with Spirits
- ☐ Cooking with Fresh Herbs
- ☐ Cooking with Cider
- ☐ Citrus! Citrus! Citrus!
- ☐ Cherries! Cherries! Cherries!
- ☐ Cooking with Garlic
- ☐ Michigan Cooking
- ☐ Minnesota Cookin'
- ☐ Missouri Cookin'
- ☐ New Jersey Cooking
- ☐ New Mexico Cooking
- ☐ New York Cooking
- ☐ Ohio Cooking
- ☐ Pennsylvania Cooking
- ☐ Wisconsin Cooking
- ☐ Amish Mennonite Apple Cookbook
- ☐ Amish Mennonite Pumpkin Cookbook
- ☐ Amish & Mennonite
- ☐ Strawberry Cookbook
- ☐ Apples Galore
- ☐ Apples! Apples! Apples!
- ☐ Berries! Berries! Berries!
- ☐ Berries Galore!
- ☐ Bountiful Blueberries
- ☐ Off To College Cookbook
- ☐ Nuts! Nuts! Nuts!
- ☐ Muffins Cookbook
- ☐ Midwest Small Town Cookin'
- ☐ Kid Pumpkin Fun Book
- ☐ Kid Money
- ☐ Kid Fun
- ☐ Kid Cookin'
- ☐ How to Make Salsa
- ☐ Holiday & Get-together Cookbook
- ☐ Hill Country Cookin'
- ☐ Plain People
- ☐ Good Cookin' From the
- ☐ Crockpot Cookbook

In-Between Cookbooks
(5 1/2 x 8 1/2) - 150 pages - $9.95

- ☐ Amish Ladies Cookbook - Old Husbands
- ☐ Amish Ladies Cookbook - Young Husbands
- ☐ The Adaptable Apple Cookbook
- ☐ Bird Up! Pheasant Cookbook
- ☐ Breads! Breads! Breads!
- ☐ Camp Cookin'
- ☐ Civil War Cookin'
- ☐ Stories, 'n Such
- ☐ Cooking Ala Nude
- ☐ Country Cooking
- ☐ Cooking for a Crowd
- ☐ Recipes from my Amish Heritage
- ☐ The Cow Puncher's Cookbook
- ☐ Eating Ohio
- ☐ Farmers Market Indian Cookbook
- ☐ Feast of Moons Indian Cookbook
- ☐ Fire Fighters Cookbook
- ☐ Football Mom's
- ☐ Halloween Fun Book
- ☐ Herbal Cookery

☐ Working Girl Cookbook
☐ Super Simple Cookin'
☐ Squash Cookbook
☐ Some Like It Hot Pumpkins! Pumpkins! Pumpkins!
☐ Peaches! Peaches! Peaches!
☐ Veggie Talk Coloring & Story Book $6.95

- ❏ Hunting in the Nude Cookbook
- ❏ Ice Cream Cookbook
- ❏ Indian Cooking Cookbook
- ❏ Little 'Ol Blue-Haired Church-Lady Cookbook
- ❏ Mad About Garlic
- ❏ Make the Play All-Sport Cookbook
- ❏ Motorcycler's Wild Critter Cookbook
- ❏ Outdoor Cooking for Outdoor Men
- ❏ Shhh Cookbook
- ❏ Soccer Mom's Cookbook

- ❏ Southwest Ghost Town Cookbook
- ❏ Turn of the Century Cooking
- ❏ Vegan Vegetarian Cookbook
- ❏ Venison Cookbook

Biggie Cookbooks
(5 1/2 x 8 1/2) - 200 plus pages - $11.95
- ❏ A Cookbook for them what Ain't Done a Whole lot of Cookin'
- ❏ Aphrodisiac Cooking
- ❏ Back to the Supper Table Cookbook
- ❏ Cooking for One (ok, Maybe two)

- ❏ Covered Bridges Cookbook
- ❏ Depression Times Cookbook
- ❏ Dial-a-Dream Cookbook
- ❏ Flat Out, Dirt Cheap Cookin'
- ❏ Hormone Helper Cookbook
- ❏ Real Men Cook on Sunday Cookbook
- ❏ The I-got-Funner-things-to do Cookbook
- ❏ Victorian Sunday Dinners

HEARTS 'N TUMMIES COOKBOOK CO.
1854 - 345th Avenue
Wever, Iowa 52658
1-800-571-BOOK

Name _____

Address _____

_____

*You Iowa folks gotta kick in another 6% for Sales Tax.